Foolproof
Walking-Foot
QUILTING DESIGNS

Visual Guide • Idea Book

Mary Mashuta

C&T PUBLISHING

Text and photography copyright © 2015 by Mary Mashuta

Photography and artwork copyright © 2015 by C&T Publishing, Inc.

Publisher: Amy Marson

Creative Director: Gailen Runge

Art Director/Cover Designer: Kristy Zacharias

Editor: Liz Aneloski

Technical Editors: Doreen Hazel and Alison M. Schmidt

Book Designer: Katie McIntosh

Production Coordinator: Zinnia Heinzmann

Production Editor: Alice Mace Nakanishi

Illustrator: Jessica Jenkins

Photo Assistant: Mary Peyton Peppo

Photography by Mary Mashuta and Diane Pedersen, unless otherwise noted

Published by C&T Publishing, Inc., P.O. Box 1456, Lafayette, CA 94549

Library of Congress Cataloging-in-Publication Data

Mashuta, Mary.

   Foolproof walking-foot quilting designs : visual guide - idea book / Mary Mashuta.

      pages cm

   Includes bibliographical references.

   ISBN 978-1-61745-051-8 (soft cover)

   1. Machine quilting--Patterns. I. Title.

TT835.M38429 2015

746.46--dc23

                                        2014047452

Printed in China

10 9 8 7 6 5 4 3 2 1

This book is
dedicated to three women:

Liz Aneloski, my editor,
who is always calm and soothing;

Rebecca Rohrkaste, who has been
my assistant for many years;

And Roberta Horton, my sister,
who always has another "right" way
of doing everything.

Contents

Let's Get Started

When I became a quilter in the early 1970s, hardly any quilting books or magazines were available. Quilters today are very lucky because just the opposite is true, to say nothing of what is also available on the Internet. When I look at a new book, I wonder if there is going to be something new and whether I will be entertained.

I have already written one book about machine quilting with a walking foot: *Foolproof Machine Quilting*. Believe it or not, I have more to say.

Who Is This Book For?

I am writing for multiple audiences:

- Beginners who have never machine quilted

- Those who never got beyond stitching in-the-ditch and straight lines with a walking foot and don't know there is more that they can do

- Those who have tried free-motion quilting and been frustrated because it takes so long to master

- Those who enjoyed *Foolproof Machine Quilting* and are eager for more information and ideas

As a professionally trained teacher, I also know that there are three kinds of readers:

- Those who read every word

- Those who are only interested in the pictures

- Those who look at the pictures, but if they find an interesting one will read the nearby text

Hopefully I have included something for all of you. Be willing to try new things rather than just repeating old designs you have already conquered.

Looking for Inspiration

Let's begin with making sure you are looking for new quilting designs wherever you go. Many of you always have a camera phone with you, so there is no excuse for missing a good shot.

I have included some pictures from my travels with my sister, Roberta Horton, who is also a quilter. She is the official family photographer, but she does let me tell her when I want a picture. Any of these pictures could be the starting point for a new quilting design. I actually used the picture of hotel carpeting in Paris, France (page 8), as inspiration for one of the borders in *Tropical Delight* (page 75).

Part of the secret is keeping your eyes constantly on alert for quilting ideas—everywhere, not just at quilt stores and quilt shows. By the way, the sidewalk painting (below) was photographed a few blocks from my house on a walk to my favorite restaurant.

The Adirondacks, New York

New Year's chalk sidewalk painting.
Berkeley, California

The Adirondacks, New York

Chapter 1 photos by Roberta Horton, unless otherwise noted

The Adirondacks, New York

Dublin, Ireland

The Adirondacks, New York

Dublin, Ireland

Chester, Great Britain

The Royal Pavilion. Brighton, Great Britain

Bridge. Paris, France

Hand-painted wall. Llanidloes, Wales

The Eiffel Tower. Paris, France

Giverny, France

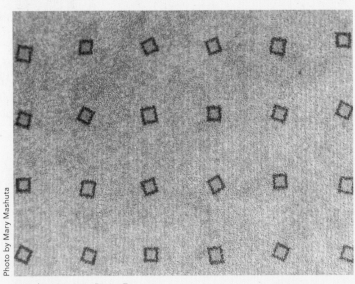

Photo by Mary Mashuta

Hotel carpeting. Paris, France

Wall decoration. Écomusée d'Alsace, France

Wall decoration. Écomusée d'Alsace, France

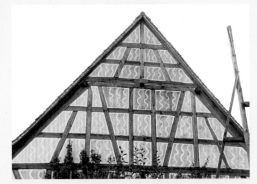

Wall decoration. Écomusée d'Alsace, France

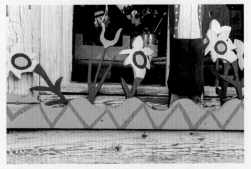

Folk art planter box. Écomusée d'Alsace, France

How to Use This Book

I have come up with a lot of possible quilting design ideas. In Chapter 3 (page 15), I will show you some great, easy ways to create quilting designs using paper folding and combining simple geometric shapes, then adapting them to stitch with a walking foot.

In Chapter 8 (page 45), I show you some simplified traditional sashiko hand-stitching designs that can also be adapted to walking-foot quilting. There are a lot to choose from.

I have devised a simple grading system of clocks to give you an idea of how complex a design is and how long it takes to stitch. One clock is simple and fast, but five clocks will take a considerable amount of time to complete.

Chapter 2

The Basics

There are benefits and drawbacks to quilting with a domestic sewing machine and a walking foot.

Benefits of Quilting with a Walking Foot

- The biggest benefit is that you can do it.

- All the stitching on the quilt is done on the right side, where you can easily see what you're doing.

- There are no pencil or chalk markings on your quilts after the quilting is finished because you make and stitch around removable templates made from self-adhesive shelf paper or freezer paper.

Note

I use Con-Tact Brand Self-Adhesive Creative Covering shelf paper for templates. You can use any brand as long as it is a solid color (not a pattern), has a paper backing you can draw on, and removes easily. You should be able to reuse your templates many times.

Reminder—don't iron the shelf paper!

- You don't have to know all the designs you want to use before you begin quilting. You can make decisions as you go.

Limitations of Quilting with a Walking Foot

- When quilting with a walking foot, you need to turn and reposition the quilt as you stitch. So, larger quilts (over 60″ × 60″) are a challenge when you use a walking foot and a regular domestic machine.

- The walking foot that works best is one made specifically for your machine, and you may need to order it. Generic ones aren't as successful but are worth a try. Some machines have a dual-feed mechanism that is already attached or built in to the machine. It is used instead of a walking foot.

Strategies for Preparing the Quilt Top

Limit your first machine-quilted project to a smaller size, so it is easier for you to handle the bulk.

Press well as you piece your quilt top to make sure all the seams are pressed in consistent directions. A final touch-up pressing may be necessary before quilting.

If there are a lot of seams at the edge of the quilt top, I always stitch all around the edge, about ⅛″ to ¼″ inside, so the seams won't come undone. However, if the quilt has unpieced borders with corner blocks, stitching ½″ across the corner-block seams is adequate.

Safety-Pin Basting a Quilt Sandwich

1. Tape backing fabric to table. Add batting. Carefully position quilt top.

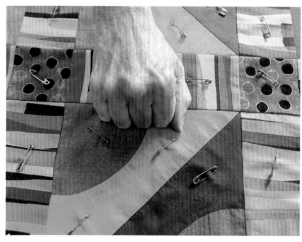

2. Place safety pins about one fist-width apart, but not near seams.

3. Close safety pins after all have been placed. A pin-closing tool helps do this.

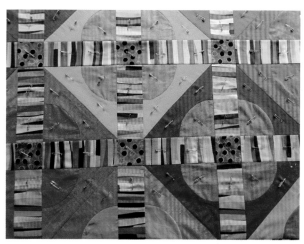

4. Pin-basted quilt top

5. As a final step, I hand baste around the quilt's edge and trim the batting and backing, so there is just ½″ extra to deal with as I quilt. (You can also see a line of machine stitching that secured the seams when the top was completed.)

A Few Notes on Supplies

- I use good-quality 50-weight cotton thread in my bobbin, no matter what weight is on the top. (Inexpensive threads don't stitch as smoothly.)

- Some 30-weight (heavier) threads can be used on the top of the machine if used with appropriate battings and needles.

- All the quilts in this book were quilted with one of my favorite 30-weight threads, either YLI Jeans Stitch (polyester) or Aurifil Cotton Mako 12, on the top of the machine. These threads really show up well. When I combine these threads with appropriate battings and needles and a longer-than-normal stitch length (approximately 8 stitches per inch), I get beautiful stitches. It's almost magic!

- I do stitching in-the-ditch with 50-weight thread and approximately 10 stitches per inch (a bit longer than for normal piecing). The walking foot works more smoothly with this longer stitch length.

- Needles with a sharp point make your stitching straighter. I use a size 11 quilting needle or size 12 jeans needle with 50-weight thread for stitching in-the-ditch and basic quilting.

- With 30-weight threads, I use a size 16 top-stitching needle, which has a sharp point and the largest eye available, for the heavier thread to pass through.

- My favorite batting is Quilters Dream Cotton. It comes in different thicknesses. I prefer the loft called Request, which is the thinnest. I also use Warm and Natural Needled Cotton Batting (by The Warm Company) or Hobbs Heirloom Premium 80/20 Cotton Blend (developed with Harriet Hargrave; works best if you presoak it). Other combinations of thread, batting, and needles may not work.

Hints for Stitching

- Make a stitching sample before you begin quilting; tension adjustments may be necessary. This is really important with the 30-weight threads.

- Many quilters are afraid to play with the tension on their machines. With 30-weight thread, you'll most often loosen the top tension. Try half steps. If loosening the tension doesn't work, try tightening it slightly.

- If you're having trouble getting nice stitches with the heavier thread, rethread the machine. You may not have gotten it seated properly in the tension mechanism.

- Always bring up the bobbin thread when you start stitching. Put both threads underneath the walking foot and hold them as you start slowly stitching.

Bring bobbin thread to top.

- To secure 50-weight thread, I reduce my stitch length and stitch about ⅛" to ¼" at the beginning and end of my quilting. I use this securing stitch when my stitching ends at the edge of the quilt top, or I hide the securing stitches near a crossing seam.

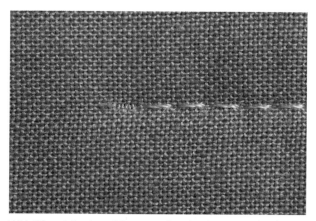

With 50-weight thread, begin and end with tiny stitches.

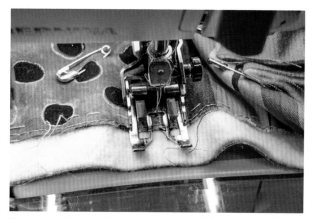

Securing with tiny stitches at edge of quilt

- You can't use a securing stitch with the heavier threads (such as 30-weight) because the short-length stitching shows too much. So I always leave 4″ lengths of top and bottom threads at the beginning and end of my stitching. These thread ends are brought to the back of the quilt and knotted off; the tails are then buried between the quilt layers, as is done in hand quilting.

- Practice sewing at a smooth, moderate speed. Avoid jerky stops and starts and fast sewing.

Strategies for Stitching in-the-Ditch

- Machine quilters often roll their basted quilt to get the bulk of the quilt out of the way of their stitching. They often balance the rolled portion over their shoulder, which isn't ideal ergonomically. As much as possible, I try to roll the portion of the top I'm trying to get out of the way and place the excess in my lap rather than over my shoulder. Smaller quilts make this easier.

Rolled quilt top

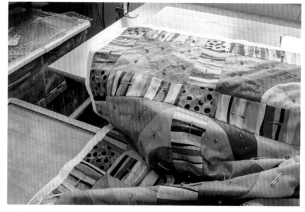

Quilt top in my lap with overflow caught on TV tray beside my machine table

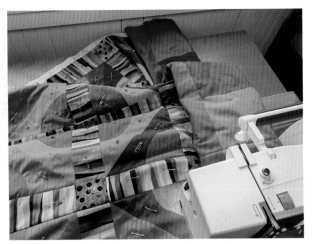

When the quilt passes under the needle, it gathers on the back of my table, which is pushed against the wall to support the quilt's weight.

- Stitch as close to the seam as possible, on the side with no seam allowances. (I press sashing seam allowances toward the sashing.)

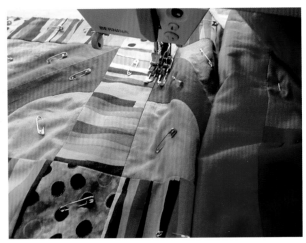

Stitch in-the-ditch close to seam.

- Make sure you stitch only where there is a seam. This means that you need to think ahead when you are pressing the top.

- To begin, stitch one line of in-the-ditch quilting vertically by the seam (not in it!) that is in (or near) the center of the quilt. Then stitch one line horizontally to intersect the first line of stitching in (or near) the middle of the quilt. Many of my quilts have sashing and borders, so this is easy. You may have a different layout, so you will have to improvise.

Decorative Stitches

Many sewing machines have decorative stitches, but it's necessary to enlarge them if you are using 30-weight threads. The regular zigzag stitch and the sewn-out zigzag are the basic decorative stitches that can be enlarged in width and length on almost all machines. The sewn-out zigzag (also called a multistep zigzag) has two or three stitches between each point and is often used to sew elastic to a garment.

Strategies for Quilting Design Motifs

- When hand quilting, you were taught to quilt from the center out. However, when machine quilting with a walking foot, you can begin anywhere once the basic stitching in-the-ditch is done and the edge of the quilt is secured. It is okay to begin with the border design.

- When stitching repeat block designs, stitch those nearest to the edge first. Build up your skill before trying the blocks in the center. It is hardest to stitch in the middle of the quilt because of the fabric bulk.

Chapter 3

Creating Quilting Designs

Learn to use your imagination to come up with quilting designs. The quilts in this book will help inspire you. Limit yourself to simple designs if you are a beginner.

Once you know what design you want to use and where you want to use it, trace it on Con-Tact or freezer paper and cut it out. Usually, it is only necessary to make one template for the quilting, because that template can be used over and over.

Designs become more complex when a second design is overlaid or additional mirroring lines are added. I save old templates to audition designs on my quilts. Then, I can reuse or modify the size as necessary when I make new templates.

Commercial Templates

Learn to look at commercial templates at quilt shops, shows, and online. Those that work best for walking-foot quilting are simple and have long continuous lines of stitching that don't overlap. You can transfer the image to Con-Tact or freezer paper and cut them out to create a template. (All the commercial templates shown in this book are from The Stencil Company, quiltingstencils.com.)

Paper-Folding Quilt Designs

Many of my motifs are paper folded. They are much simpler than the snowflakes you cut as a child. Simple paper-folded quilting motifs are easy to cut.

Each design in this section is based on a square folded four times. Start with a square piece of paper the size you want your design to be.

Fold 1: Fold square of paper in half.

Fold 2: Fold in half again.

Fold 3: Fold top section of square diagonally to front.

Fold 4: Fold remaining section diagonally to back.

1.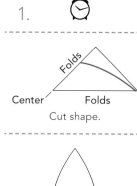
Cut shape.
Completed shape

2.
Cut shape.
Completed shape

3.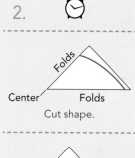
Cut shape.
Completed shape

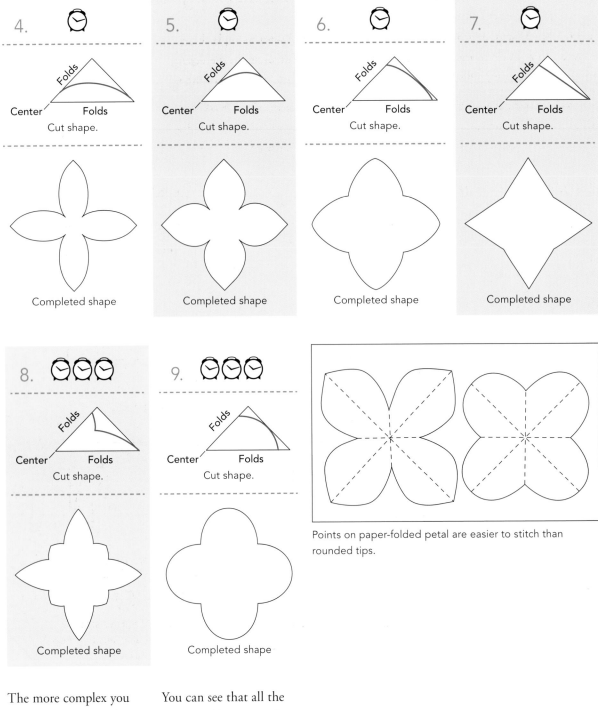

4.

Folds

Center Folds

Cut shape.

Completed shape

5.

Folds

Center Folds

Cut shape.

Completed shape

6.

Folds

Center Folds

Cut shape.

Completed shape

7.

Folds

Center Folds

Cut shape.

Completed shape

8.

Folds

Center Folds

Cut shape.

Completed shape

9.

Folds

Center Folds

Cut shape.

Completed shape

Points on paper-folded petal are easier to stitch than rounded tips.

The more complex you make the design with extra pivots, the harder it is to stitch. Think "less is more." If you want more complexity, you can add a second motif on top of the first or add outline stitching.

You can see that all the previous illustrations have definite points rather than rounded points at the petal tips. It is much easier to stop, pivot, and resume stitching than it is to try and take several smooth stitches in a curved point.

Using Geometric Shapes for Quilt Designs

Many geometric shapes are suitable for a quilting design. Start with a simple shape; then rotate and repeat it to make the design more complex. The more detailed the design, the more pivoting will be required, and the design will take longer to stitch.

When making your decision about the design's complexity, decide where it will be located on the quilt, how large it will be, and how many times you will be repeating it. And, of course, consider your skill level and the time commitment.

Expanding Simple Triangles

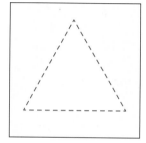

Single triangle

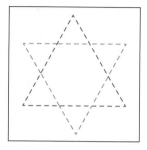

Two stacked triangles stitched separately (6 points, 4 pivots)

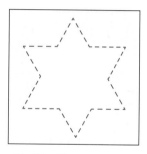

Two stacked triangles stitched around outer edge to make six-point figure (6 points, 11 pivots)

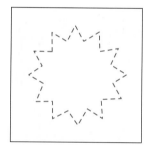

Two stacked six-point figures (12 points, 23 pivots)

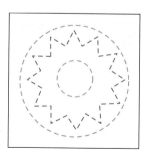

Twelve-point figure with inner and outer circles added

Expanding a Square

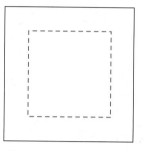

Single square

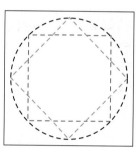

Two stacked squares stitched separately inside stitched circle (8 points, 6 pivots)

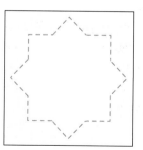

Two stacked squares stitched around outside edge only (8 points, 15 pivots)

Expanding a Four-Point Star

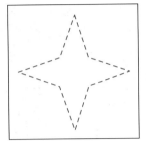

Four-point star

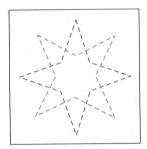

Two stacked four-point stars stitched separately (8 points, 14 pivots)

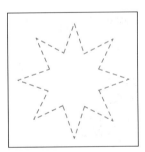

Two stacked four-point stars stitched around outer edge only (8 points, 15 pivots)

Expanding a Five-Point Star

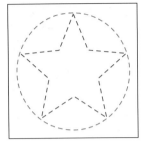

Five-point star within circle

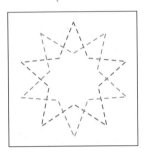

Two stacked five-point stars stitched separately (10 points, 18 pivots)

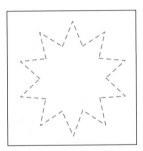

Two stacked five-point stars stitched around outer edge only (10 points, 19 pivots)

Coming Up with New Designs

Quilting all the blocks differently lets you experiment and forces you to stretch and come up with new designs. Examples from the *Sampler Quilt* (full quilt, page 61) will give you some ideas.

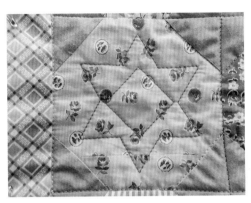

Square added to stacked triangles

Second square added to center

A twelve-point figure with a center circle has a lot of pivots and requires a bit more skill, patience, and time.

Chapter 4:

Quilting Blocks

Most of my quilts are made from traditional pieced blocks. I opt for fewer pieces rather than more, because I like to show off my fabrics and machine-quilting designs. Sometimes I consider the piecing pattern when creating a design. Other times, I superimpose a new quilting design over the whole block. And sometimes I can even stitch from one block into the next.

I always make sure I have stitched in-the-ditch around the edge of the block with 50-weight thread. I may also outline some of the piecing. The decorative motifs are stitched with 30-weight thread, unless otherwise noted.

Traditional blocks are fun to use in new ways. Here are some great ways to quilt them. Use these ideas as inspiration for your blocks.

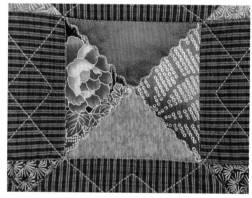

- Seams pressed open and overlaid with decorative quilting stitch
- 50-weight thread
- *Japanese Treasure Chest* (full quilt, page 60)

Basket

- Striped fabrics provide lines to create chevron stitching in basket body.
- Handle highlighted with decorative stitch
- Background mirror stitched using edge of walking foot
- *Mary's Adirondack Baskets* (full quilt, page 54)

Pizza

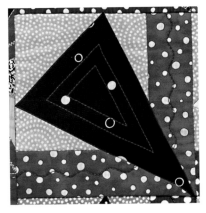

- Triangle stitching within triangle. (Mark the midpoints of each side of the triangle with a pin. Place painter's tape between the two pinned points and stitch. Rotate, move tape, and stitch in the next direction.)
- Outline stitching on two inside border edges
- *Japanese Pizza I* (full quilt, page 63)

- Two triangles nestled in large triangle (Create a template to stitch around by trimming a paper tracing of a triangle template. Or you can use the edge of your walking foot as a guide. Stitch the larger triangle first and the center smaller one inside.)
- Decorative stitch centered in two borders
- *Black and White Dot Pizza* (full quilt, page 62)

- Four-petal flower motif (see Paper-Folding Quilt Designs, page 16) with button embellishment
- Narrow outline stitching mirrors point of triangle and inside edges of border
- *Japanese Pizza II* (full quilt, page 63)

Sometimes the individual blocks join to become a larger unit.

- Four-petal motif (see Paper-Folding Quilt Designs, page 16) in center space
- Simple oval leaves with curved vein down center within triangles
- *Dutch Pizza* (full quilt, page 65)

- Two stacked four-petal motifs (see Paper-Folding Quilt Designs, page 16) with mirror stitching around entire new motif
- Yo-yo draws eye to center of new design.
- *Indian Pizza* (full quilt, page 64)

Curved Bowtie

- Two stacked four-petal motifs (see Paper-Folding Quilt Designs, page 16)
- Folded origami biscuit puff in center
- *Christmas Curved Bowtie* (full quilt, page 58)

Propeller

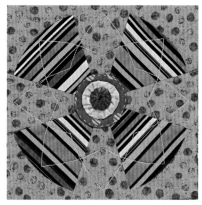

- Two stacked four-petal motifs
- Two fun, stacked yo-yos added to center circle
- Center circle hand stitched with 30-weight thread so stitching stands out
- *Long Beach Propellers* (full quilt, page 67)

- Two different stacked motifs on block
- Center includes rickrack
- 30-weight blanket stitching, hand stitching, and yo-yo.
- *Bouquet for Usha* (full quilt, page 66)

- Two stacked four-petal motifs
- One petal motif mirror stitched and partial circles added
- *Sayonara Gaigin* (full quilt, page 68)

Circle Within a Circle

- Two stacked four-petal motifs in center
- Pointed scalloped edging around outside of circle to fill negative space
- (Template was made by paper folding (page 15) photocopy of block to create design and then transferring it to Con-Tact paper.)
- *Thank You Mood* (full quilt, page 57)

- Scallop stitching in middle of circle segments (I paper folded one segment and cut symmetrical curves to make template. I made six individual templates rather than one continuous one because it worked better with seams between segments.)
- Mirror-stitched scallop using edge of walking foot as guide, pivoting slightly when needed (needle always in down position)
- *Bouquet for Gloria* (full quilt, page 56)

- Two lines of curved quilting inside segments mirror block's curves
- Stitch using guide that attaches to walking foot. (It is easiest to stitch both rows from larger curve because stitching will be smoother with less pivoting.)
- Negative space filled with plain and decorative quilting using same attachment
- *Beamish Woman* (full quilt, page 65)

Stitching Using a Guide

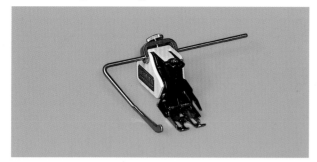

Position seam guide to right or left of walking foot. Run edge of guide along line you wish to mirror.

EXAMPLE A

1. Attached seam guide allows you to evenly stitch continuous line from outside edge of curve, from wedge to wedge.

2. Lengthening bar of attached seam guide lets you stitch evenly near block's inside curve.

EXAMPLE B

1. Pivot point for line of straight curved stitching that mirrors decorative-stitch quilting

2. Negative space filled in with more curved quilting

Wagon Wheel

- Yo-yo with button in center
- First row of straight stitching in hexagon shape
- Painter's tape used to mark lines of stitching
- *Wheels for Usha* (full quilt, page 77)

- Second row of straight mirror stitching inside hexagon
- *Wheels for Usha* (full quilt, page 77)

- Yo-yo with button in center
- Circle template with center cut out so it will lie flat
- *Wheels for Usha* (full quilt, page 77)

- Yo-yo with button in center
- Circle template was stitched around outside edge only.
- Second circle was mirror stitched around inside of first circle using seam guide attached to walking foot.
- *Wheels for Usha* (full quilt, page 77)

- Yo-yo with button in center
- This variation combines both circles and straight lines.
- *Wheels for Usha* (full quilt, page 77)

- Same template method used where partial blocks run into border
- Appliquéd circle overlapping into border
- *Wheels for Usha* (full quilt, page 77)

- Touching same-stripe spokes are outline quilted as one piece, rather than two separate pieces, using edge of walking foot
- Yo-yo in center of block
- *Wheels for Mary Bozak* (full quilt, page 76)

Swirling Petals

- Black interior stitching in petals using edge of walking foot
- Blanket stitch quilting around petals
- Light-colored stitching in curved triangle negative space using edge of walking foot
- Black blanket stitch quilting around petals actually continues from one block to next, as does outline in negative space.
- *Tropical Delight* (full quilt, page 75)

- Negative space was stitched in one continuous line, using guide attached to walking foot to create large circle as quilt was rotated.
- Two crisscrossing, very simple pointed ellipses were stitched in white over block intersections. The eye goes there immediately.
- *Fruit Delight* (full quilt, page 71)

- Two different four-petal designs (see Paper-Folding Quilt Designs, pages 15 and 16) tailored to dimensions of block and stacked to fill spaces
- Origami biscuit puff in center square
- *Indonesian Swirling Petals* (full quilt, page 72)

Circle X

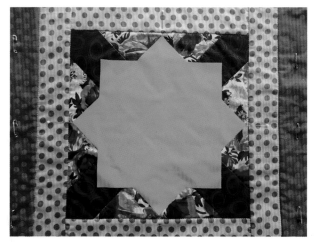

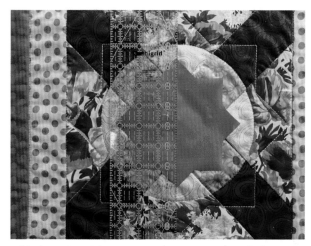

- Largest eight-point shape (see Expanding a Square, page 17) was created by stacking two squares on top of each other, rotating second square one-half turn, then transferring design onto Con-Tact or freezer paper.
- *Circle X* (full quilt, page 65)

- Medium-size eight-point template centered inside first eight-point shape
- *Circle X* (full quilt, page 65)

- Small eight-point template centered inside second eight-point shape.
- *Circle X* (full quilt, page 65)

- Mirror stitching around largest eight-point shape
- *Circle X* (full quilt, page 65)

Around the Twist

- Double-line grid quilting pattern (Painter's tape was used to connect lines in piecing pattern to create allover double-line grid pattern.)
- Decorative stitch used between double vertical lines
- *Barcelona Twist* (full quilt, page 53)

Serpentine Curves

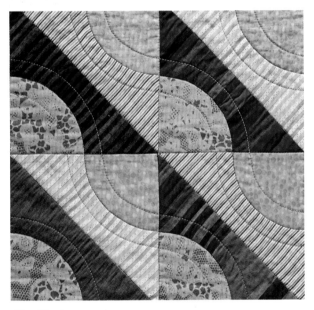

- Outline stitching on both sides of diagonal curves using attached seam guide
- *Diagonal Serpentine Curves* (full quilt, page 69)

- Two eight-point shapes (see Expanding a Square, page 17) are stitched in four-block intersections. Larger shape is stitched first; then second one inside it.
- Third, small, eight-point octagon is stitched in minor intersections.
- Block curves are stitched in-the-ditch separately, but long lines of diagonal stitching across diagonal seams of blocks could continue through sashing posts and onto next block seam for very efficient stitching.
- *Sashed Serpentine Curves* (full quilt, page 70)

Chapter 5

Quilting Center Panels

I have made five quilts that feature a center panel. They are quite different from each other, but each presents a new challenge to try something different.

- Double straight lines using ¾″ painter's tape alternate with wave-pattern quilting lines from commercial template traced onto Con-Tact paper and cut out. For making your own wave template, see Tip (page 41).
- *Sayonara Gaigin* (full quilt, page 68)

- Horizontal/vertical grid quilting was stitched before appliqué pieces were added. The appliqué pieces are all double thickness so that the quilting lines won't show through them.
- *Glove Quilt* (full quilt, page 78)

- Diagonal grid quilting stitched after vase was added
- Crochet motifs ("flowers") added after quilting
- Button embellishment
- *Bouquet for Usha* (full quilt, page 66)

- Quilting on printed lines
- 50-weight thread
- *Beamish Woman* (full quilt, page 55)

- Basic outline quilting for vase and preprinted flowers
- Glove, crocheted pieces, button, and French knots embellishment
- *Bouquet for Gloria* (full quilt, page 56)

Chapter 6

Quilting in Supportive Spaces

Some parts of the quilt are less important than others, even though they all add to the total composition. These supportive spaces can be the sashing between blocks, narrow borders separating parts of the quilt, alternate plain blocks, and corner blocks.

Sashing

After the quilt is safety-pin basted, I always stitch in-the-ditch on both sides of my sashing and narrow borders. Sometimes that is enough quilting in these areas, particularly when I'm in a hurry.

The main limitation of sashing strips is their relatively small size. Shorter lengths can mean a lot of stops and starts, unless you can figure out a way to keep going with your stitching.

- Curved sashing embellished with both machine stitching and handwork, including French knots on rickrack trim
- *Curved Bowtie 3* (full quilt, page 59)

- Straight and zigzag stitching
- Rickrack embellished with small beads
- *Christmas Curved Bowtie* (full quilt, page 58)

Curved Stitching Using a Template

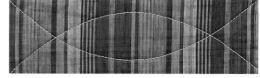

- Two simple curves intersect in sashing unit
- *Long Beach Propellers* (full quilt, page 67)

Cut a piece of paper the size of the finished sashing unit. Fold it in half vertically (the short way), and cut a simple curve from the fold to the opposite corner.

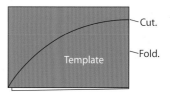

Fold paper and cut template.

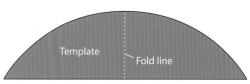

Use template as guide for stitching.

I stitched the template twice, so each unit has a right-side-up curve and an upside-down curve. One stitched curve is on top of the other.

To keep from having to work in so many ends, stitch the curves from one segment to another as you turn the quilt at right angles. You will need a minimum of two templates to alternate as you stitch from segment to segment. It is important to learn to see how far you can go before you stop stitching.

Stitch one continuous circular shape around center block.

Straight Stitching in Pieced Sashing

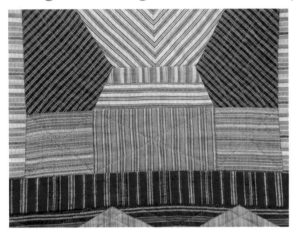

- Two lines of straight stitching diagonally crisscross the sashing (marked with painter's tape before stitching)
- *Mary's Adirondack Basket* (full quilt, page 54)

Triangle Stitching Using a Template

Oops! Opposite points are not even.

Be sure that opposite points of triangle templates are placed across from each other. Place pin at midpoint of sashing piece to ensure accurate pivots.

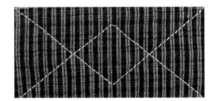

- Double triangles stitched using triangle templates in rectangular sashing pieces
- See how far you can stitch before you stop (see Curved Stitching Using a Template, page 31).
- *Japanese Treasure Chest* (full quilt, page 60)

Borders

An important part of the quilt that we don't often think about is the narrow border that divides the parts of the quilt from each other.

Unpieced Narrow Borders

- Simple zigzag, straight-line stitching using painter's tape as guide
- *Sayonara Gaigin* (full quilt, page 68)

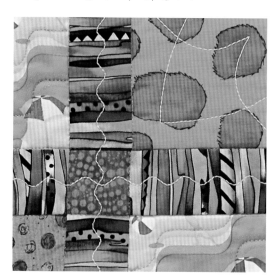

- Decorative stitching
- *Long Beach Propellers* (full quilt, page 67)

Note

Learn to look at commercial quilting templates at quilt shops and shows or shop online. (All the commercial templates shown in this book are from The Stencil Company, quiltingstencils.com.) Some templates can be used for machine quilting after being transferred to Con-Tact or freezer paper and cut out. For you to be able to stitch continuously, you must create a new template that is long enough to reach from one end of the quilting area to the other.

Enlarge or reduce size and length of design as needed to turn corners evenly.

- Carefully peel off Con-Tact paper template after stitching is completed.
- *Circle X* (full quilt, page 65)

- Commercial wave stencil embellished with decorative stitching
- *Bouquet for Gloria* (full quilt, page 56)

Pieced Narrow Borders

Pieced narrow borders can be more interesting than plain ones. Remember to see how far you can stitch without stopping.

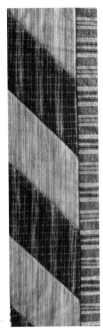

- Straight-line quilting
- Concentrate on continuously stitching as you cross quilt. Walking-foot edge will help guide you when it is time to pivot.
- *Mary's Adirondack Baskets* (full quilt, page 54)

- Cheater" rectangle at center of pieced narrow border makes it correct length.
- *Mary's Adirondack Baskets* (full quilt, page 54)

- Stitched in-the-ditch along diagonal lines (a lot of starts and stops)
- *Mary's Adirondack Baskets* (full quilt, page 54)

Corner Blocks

Most of my bordered quilts have corner blocks, which eliminate the need to come up with a quilting design that goes around the corner. It's also easy to reach the blocks when it's time to quilt them, since they are at the quilt's edge.

Corners are a perfect area to place more elaborate paper-folded designs (page 16). You can also challenge yourself to come up with four different corner designs.

- Machine- and hand-quilted paisley design inspired by print fabric
- *Diagonal Serpentine Curves* (full quilt, page 69)

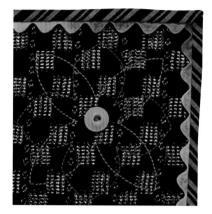

- Two different four-petal motifs (see Paper-Folding Quilting Designs, pages 15 and 16) stacked and stitched in different colors
- Button embellishment
- *Japanese Pizza II* (full quilt, page 63)

- Five-petal flower machine and hand stitched (Note that small rounded corners are harder to machine stitch than pointed corners.)
- Embellished with two stacked yo-yos
- *Indian Pizza* (full quilt, page 64)

- Stacked four-petal motif (See Paper-Folding Quilting Designs, pages 15 and 16.)
- Yo-yo is added to center and eight tiny buttons are sewn onto petals.
- *Black and White Dot Pizza* (full quilt, page 62)

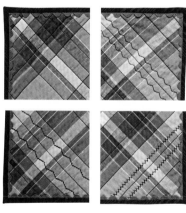

- Straight and decorative stitching
- *Tropical Delight* (full quilt, page 75)

- Off-center circle design with three stacked circles of different sizes
- (Stitch largest circle first.)
- Graduated circle templates (Karen Kay Buckley's Bigger Perfect Circles, karenkaybuckley.com)
- *Sampler Quilt* (full quilt, page 61)

- Five-point star in circle with mirrored lines (adds starts and stops but makes design more interesting)
- *Sampler Quilt* (full quilt, page 61)

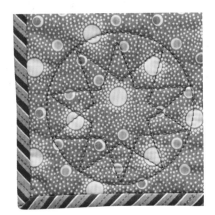

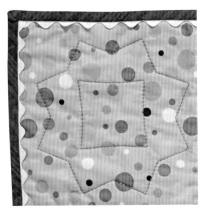

- Five-point stars stacked in circle
- *Sampler Quilt* (full quilt, page 61)

- Ten-point motif with center circle
- (To create template, trace around two stacked templates, transfer to Con-Tact or freezer paper, and cut out.)
- *Sampler Quilt* (full quilt, page 61)

- Eight-point motif with small center square
- *Fruit Delight* (full quilt, page 71)

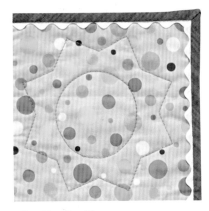

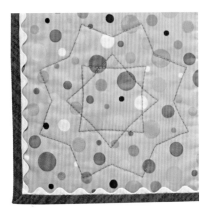

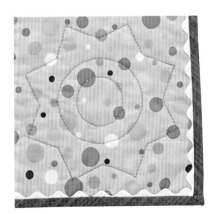

- Eight-point motif with small center circle
- *Fruit Delight* (full quilt, page 71)

- Eight-point motif with two center squares
- *Fruit Delight* (full quilt, page 71)

- Eight-point motif with two center circles
- *Fruit Delight* (full quilt, page 71)

Chapter 7

Border Quilting Designs

The majority of my quilts have unpieced print borders. Even though I am concentrating on quilt borders here, you may find other large areas on your quilts where these techniques would work.

Letting the Print Determine the Quilting

Some prints are perfect candidates for borders because their impact might be lost if they were cut up in small pieces.

Most beginning machine quilters would look at the banana and leaf print that borders *Tropical Delight* (full quilt, page 75) and say, "I can quilt around the motifs." But what looks obvious is also time-consuming and has a lot of twists and turns, to say nothing about the numerous ends to work in after a section is completed.

But, there were a lot of ends to work in with heavy thread (see Hints for Stitching, page 12).

- Fabric print outline quilted
- 30-weight thread
- *Tropical Delight* (full quilt, page 75)

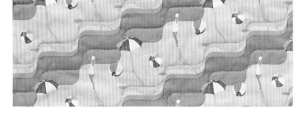

- Quilting follows undulating lines in print.
- 50-weight thread
- *Long Beach Propellers* (full quilt, page 67)

- Diagonal quilting lines
- Yo-yo and button embellishments
- 30-weight thread
- *Indonesian Swirling Petals* (full quilt, page 72)

- Hand and machine quilting
- Background of border filled in with elongated decorative stitch (complicated, but worth it)
- 50-weight thread
- *Diagonal Serpentine Curves* (full quilt, page 69)

- Simple four-petal flower design (see Paper-Folding Quilt Designs, page 16) repeated on border fabric and continued around corner blocks
- Bead and button embellishments
- *Curved Bowtie 3* (full quilt, page 59)

- Simple curves are fast and easy to mirror using walking foot and seam guide.
- *Curved Bowtie 2* (full quilt, page 59)

- Let fabric print tell you where to machine or hand quilt.
- Button embellishment
- *Black and White Dot Pizza* (full quilt, page 62)

- Machine straight and decorative stitches, along with hand-embroidered stitches, follow circular fabric pattern.
- *Swirling Circles and Stripes* (full quilt, page 74)

Quilting Motifs over Print Fabrics

Quilting a design over print fabrics can be a challenge, but here are some great ideas.

Using Simple Shapes

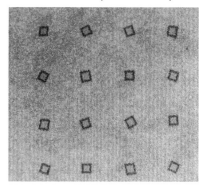

Paris hotel carpet inspiration.
Paris, France

- Random squares quilted over print fabric (They are fast and easy. Overlapping some squares makes quilting more playful.)
- *Tropical Delight* (full quilt, page 75)

Using Template Motifs

1. Scallop extends from midpoint of one triangle to midpoint of next triangle.

2. Enough Con-Tact paper templates are cut to reach from one end of the border to the other.

3. Stitching right at edge of templates

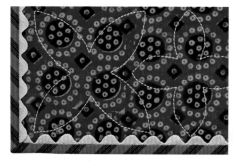

- Two simple four-petal paper-folded motifs (see Paper-Folding Quilt Designs, pages 15 and 16) repeated on border
- *Wheels for Usha* (full quilt, page 77)

- Two narrow borders treated as one design area with motifs centered on seamline
- *Wheels for Usha* (full quilt, page 77)

Cables

Students love my cables because they are fast and easy. Paper cut a pointed oval, transfer to Con-Tact or freezer paper, and cut it out. You need enough templates to fill your border length.

Place the motifs with a ⅛″ gap between them; then serpentine stitch (switching from one side to the other) down each side of the lined-up ovals. Once the basic outlines are stitched, you can add additional stitching.

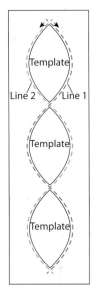

Serpentine stitch between ovals, switching from side to side.

- Black serpentine stitching creates cable.
- Additional lines mirror stitched on each side of cable

- Black serpentine stitching creates cable.
- Decorative stitching added to mirror cable

- Pieced border, with different thread colors to match each segment
- *Dutch Pizza* (full quilt, page 65)

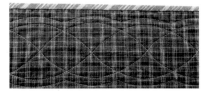

- Offset serpentine cable (basic cable with second cable staggered)
- Mirror stitching added to fill border
- *Mary's Adirondack Baskets* (full quilt, page 54)

- Offset serpentine cable (basic cable with second cable staggered so that lines cross in middle of first cable)
- Button embellishment
- *Indian Pizza* (full quilt, page 64)

An interesting variation is possible when you add on-point squares between the basic oval cable shapes. Again, you serpentine stitch the ovals. However, it is necessary to stop and pivot on each square to change direction. Additional lines can be added, but decorative stitches don't work, because you can't predict where the pivot will occur in the design.

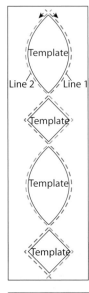

Serpentine stitch around oval and pivot on square to change direction.

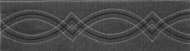

Cable with on-point squares

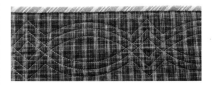

- Squares are added to basic cable.
- Mirror stitching added to fill border
- *Mary's Adirondack Baskets* (full quilt, page 54)

Commercial Template Designs

Look for commercial templates at quilt shops, shows, and online. Use ones with simple designs that have long, continuous lines of stitching that don't overlap. (All the commercial templates shown in this book are from The Stencil Company, quiltingstencils.com.) You can transfer the image to Con-Tact or freezer paper and then cut it out to create a template.

Waves

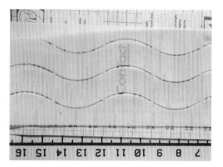

1. Trace commercial template on wrong side of Con-Tact paper cut to length of your border. (Don't use ink as it might smear on your fabric.)

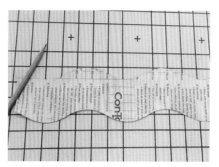

2. Cut out template and remove paper before placing template on quilt.

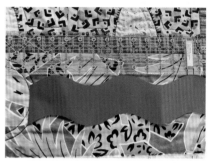

3. Carefully position template.

4. Stitch along edge of template.

5. Add decorative stitching to mirror wave design.

TIP

If you can't get a commercial template, try making enlarged copies of rickrack on your photocopy machine.

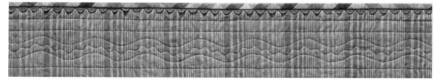

- Decorative stitching added down middle of serpentine curve for fast results
- Straight-line stitching using painter's tape as guide
- *Kaffe's Swirling Petals* (full quilt, page 73)

Baptist Fan

Note

Quilters have been using the design called Baptist Fan, Bishop's Fan, Methodist Fan, or Amish Fan as an allover quilting design for many years. You can purchase the fan templates in different sizes. Smaller Baptist Fan templates are perfect for borders and are easy to stitch, since there is just one row of the design.

Don't worry about including only complete sets of arcs. Wherever the pattern ends is where it ends.

- Additional single stitched lines added to basic Baptist Fan
- *Japanese Pizza II* (full quilt, page 63)

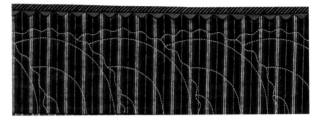

- Single line of decorative stitching added to edge of each Baptist Fan
- *Japanese Pizza I* (full quilt, page 63)

More variations

- Baptist Fan design was machine quilted one arc at a time until whole quilt was filled.
- *Not So Many Dots* (full quilt, page 61)

Note

When making a template for the Baptist Fan design, keep in mind that it is a one-way design. So if you're using Con-Tact paper, draw on the back of the template (what will be the sticky side) so your design will be reversed. With freezer paper, draw on the dull side (nontacky side) so the design will be oriented as you want it to appear on the quilt.

Challenge Yourself to Create New Border Designs

Forcing yourself to come up with four border designs, rather than one, for a quilt is a good stretch. Once your creativity is turned on, it will be easier to audition possible new designs.

Here are some examples from the quilts *Tropical Delight* (page 75) and *Fruit Delight* (page 71).

Border length divided equally—Pin marks point of pivot and makes it easy to place painter's tape to stitch straight lines for diamonds.

Possible shapes auditioned for placement in diamonds

Center of square determined—Pin helps to place center precisely between two diamonds.

On another quilt, I played with just circles and then circles with diamonds.

Possible petal motif auditioned

Circle templates placed on border

Stitched circles overlapped with more circles

Additional line of mirror stitching added to each circle

Circle added to center of diamonds—Notice how marks on template make it easy to find correct placement.

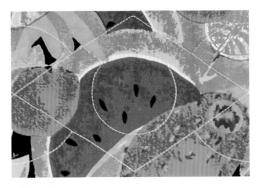

Larger partial circles added to intersecting diamonds

Decorative stitch mirrors straight-stitched partial circles

A practice quilt doesn't have to be large. *Sampler Quilt* (full quilt, page 61) is only 25″ × 25″ square, but it has nine different quilting designs in the blocks, four different designs in the corner squares, and four different quilting combinations in the borders.

Audition different designs.

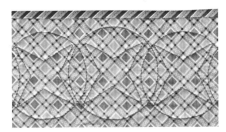

Circles within circles, using commercial circle templates

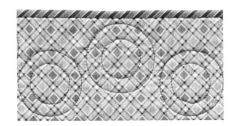

Circles in three sizes, plus stars

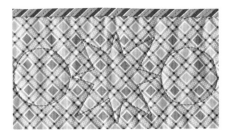

Complex stars (stacked stars in two different sizes) stitched on outside edge only, plus circles

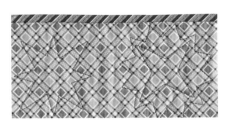 

Showing off!!

Chapter 8

Sashiko Quilting Designs

Japanese sashiko hand stitching was originally used to sew layers of fabric together to make them stronger. Over time it evolved into beautiful patterns marked on indigo and hand stitched with white thread for decorative effects.

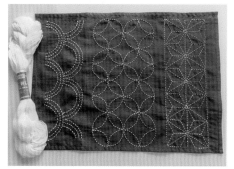

Traditional sashiko sampler of three designs by Roberta Horton, with skein of thread

As a *gaigin* (foreigner or "white devil"), I was able to look at the designs and realize that some of them could be adapted to machine walking-foot quilting. I kept saying "less is more" as I figured out how I could simplify the more complicated designs. However, if you prefer a "more is more" approach, just keep in mind that it will take longer, and there will be more ends to work in.

These designs show best on unpieced solids or on fabrics with subtle patterns. The quilt in the photographs in this chapter is *Japanese Treasure Chest* (page 60). I used a different design on each of the four borders and in each of the four border corners. Since making the quilt, I now realize that I could go even further, so I have included many additional sketches of alternate possibilities for you to try.

Diamonds: *Hishi*

This pattern is done traditionally with a diamond grid. What is important is to find some way of dividing the length and width of your area so you create a pleasing pattern of equal shapes. Painter's tape helps me stitch straight diagonal lines. I mark pivot points with a straight pin.

Use painter's tape to stitch straight lines.

You could also make your grid of squares rather than diamonds, if the height and width are equal proportions.

Square variation

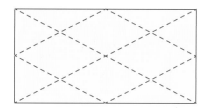

Diamonds

Diamonds

Fish Scales: *Uroko*

Adding straight lines perpendicular to the edge of a diamond grid will make the Fish Scales sashiko design. Going beyond tradition, you could also add the perpendicular lines to a grid made of on-point squares.

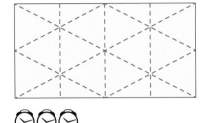

Fish Scales

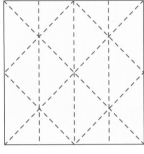

Square Fish Scales

Connected Fans: *Oogi Tsu Na Gi*

A similar but more complicated pattern substitutes zigzag stitches for the straight perpendicular stitches in the diamonds of Fish Scales. To make it even fancier, bows are added to the intersections in traditional sashiko. Again, squares, rather than diamonds, are an option if the squares fit your space better.

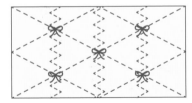

Connected Fans

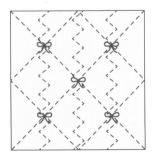

Square Connected Fans

My diamonds did end up becoming squares. Pivots were lined up with the small triangles in the pieced sashing. Then I added a second grid. This time, pivots were lined up with the midpoints of the sashing pieces.

Square grid resulted when rectangular border space was divided.

Grid is divided again. Painter's tape is lined up with pivot points, which are marked with straight pins.

Finally, I added the sewn-out zigzag stitch. It is one of the few stitches that can be enlarged on almost all zigzag machines. This is essential if you are using heavy threads. The bows were obviously not in keeping with my "less is more" approach.

Adding decorative stitch to grid

Connected Fans

Pine Tree Bark: *Matsukawa Bishi*

The other two sashiko borders were based on designs that crisscrossed diagonally, which meant they were much harder. I finally realized I could just use one direction of the patterns for simpler, do-able designs. To make a template, transfer a single line of zigzags to Con-Tact or freezer paper in preparation for stitching by machine.

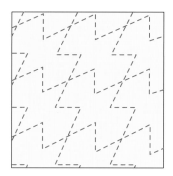

Pine Tree Bark uses diamond-shaped zigzag pattern.

Pine Tree Bark uses a diamond-shaped zigzag pattern. The zigzag can be used singly in narrow rectangles or in multiples for squares or larger rectangles. Just keep in mind that you will have to have enough units of the design to cover the distance from the top to the bottom of your shape.

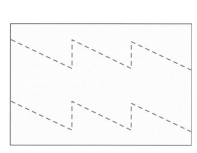

One-way Pine Tree Bark in rectangle

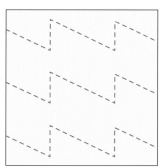

One-way Pine Tree Bark in square

I used my new Pine Tree Bark in a rectangular border, stitching one zigzag at a time. An additional line of zigzag mirror stitching was added to my one-direction design to make it more interesting. You can use the same pattern in a square just by altering the spacing to make a pleasing design.

Stitch along edge of Con-Tact paper pattern.

Add mirror stitching.

Mary's Pine Tree Bark with mirror stitching

Balance Weight: *Fun Do*

This pattern is also called Counterweights: *Fundo Tsunagi*. It was the hardest for me to draw. It is based on rows of touching circles. A second set of circles is then added by drawing new circles where four quarter circles meet in the first set. It is helpful to use a square grid as a base for drawing the circles.

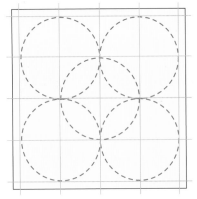

Balance Weight begins with touching circles. Second set of circles is centered where corners meet.

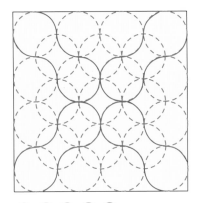

Undulating lines are connected in crisscrossing directions.

Using just one direction of the design makes this a good design for us. One line can be placed parallel to the long edge of a thin rectangle, or multiple lines can be placed in squares or larger rectangles. Again, make sure your template has enough units of the design to cover the distance from one end of your square or rectangle to the other.

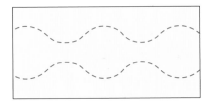

One-way Balance Weight in narrow rectangle

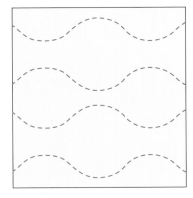

One-way Balance Weight in square

To stitch my quilt border, I used the one-way design running diagonally. I added a mirroring line to one side to make it more interesting.

Mirror stitching added to one side of each line

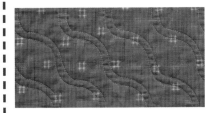

Mary's Balance Weight

The one-way Balance Weight design could also be used to set off a center square pieced block or appliqué that is the featured player, or *medallion*, in a quilt. Attach four right-angle triangles to the four edges of the block. Then decide which direction to run the one-way Balance Weight and whether the center block should be placed on-square or on-point.

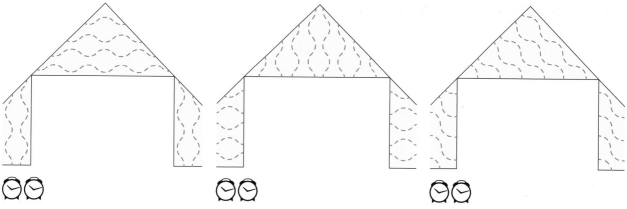

One-way Balance Weight design runs parallel to diagonal (hypotenuse) of triangles.

One-way Balance Weight design runs perpendicular to diagonal (hypotenuse) of triangles.

One-way Balance Weight design runs parallel to one right-angle edge of triangle.

I expanded my original set of four rectangular border designs so that you can now use them in other shaped rectangles, in squares, or even in triangles.

- -

Chrysanthemum: *Kiku*

When I made *Japanese Treasure Chest* (page 60) I challenged myself to create four different corner-block designs. However, I limited myself to using one traditional sashiko pattern called Chrysanthemum.

Furoshiki are traditional Japanese wrapping cloths. Duplicate scalloped quarter-circle Chrysanthemums are often repeated on the four corners. I needed four variations.

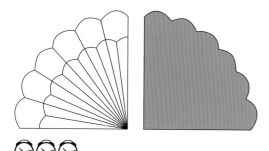

Traditional Chrysanthemum furoshiki pattern with Con-Tact paper template

The original design has spokes that connect the scallops to the right-angle corner of the quarter-circle. The point where they meet can be bulky, so this was one of the areas I concentrated on changing in some

of my new designs. In the tradition of "making do," variation A has a fabric that is slightly different from the other three corners.

I used the guide that attaches to the walking foot for both straight and decorative curves, which I added to the scallop edge.

Chrysanthemum Variation A

- Three spokes eliminated
- Partial circle and two arcs added

Chrysanthemum Variation B

- Three spokes eliminated
- Scalloped decorative stitch (BERNINA) arc and two straight-stitched arcs added

Chrysanthemum Variation C

- Three spokes eliminated
- Straight-stitch arc and scalloped decorative stitch (BERNINA) arcs added

Chrysanthemum Variation D

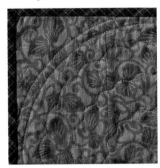

- All spokes eliminated
- Two scalloped decorative stitch (BERNINA) arcs added
- Two straight-stitch arcs added at outer edge

New Chrysanthemum Variations in a Square

Once the quilt was completed, I returned to the original Chrysanthemum design and came up with all kinds of other ways to use it. Look at the layouts, but also notice the variations in how the basic design is drawn. Feel free to mix and switch what I have drawn.

Squares were a natural place to start.

Chrysanthemum Variation in a Square A

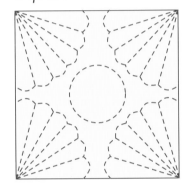

Four corner Chrysanthemums, plus center circle

Chrysanthemum Variation in a Square B

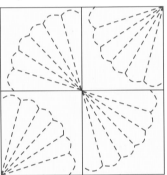

- Two opposite-corner Chrysanthemums
- Two center-pivot Chrysanthemums

Chrysanthemum Variation in a Square C

Four Chrysanthemums joined to form circle, plus inner circle, which eliminates many stitching lines meeting at single point

Chrysanthemum Variation in a Square D

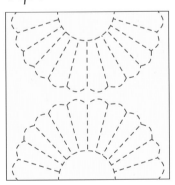

Two half-circle Chrysanthemums opposite each other

New Chrysanthemum Variations in Rectangles

Once I got warmed up, I came up with even more variations. The challenge this time was rectangles. Again, notice changes in layout and how the figures are drawn. There is really a lot of variation available to suit your abilities and time commitment.

Chrysanthemum Variation in a Rectangle A

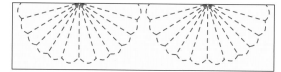

Two Chrysanthemums joined and repeated

Chrysanthemum Variation in a Rectangle B

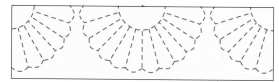

- One Chrysanthemum, plus two Chrysanthemums joined, plus one Chrysanthemum
- Inner circle added to each motif

Chrysanthemum Variation in a Rectangle C

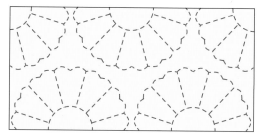

- Wider rectangle lets you switch placement of Chrysanthemums on two sides for added interest.
- Alternate spokes eliminated and inner circles added

New Chrysanthemum Variations in Triangles

Double motifs also work well in triangles. Use them to frame a pieced or appliquéd square block. Pieced borders made of triangles are another option. Alternate two solid colors with Chrysanthemums in each color, or contrast solid triangle Chrysanthemums with a print for less work.

Chrysanthemum Variation in a Triangle A

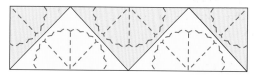

Two joined Chrysanthemums are perfect placed in triangles framing a square.

Chrysanthemum Variation in a Triangle B

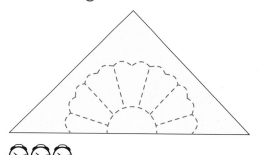

Two joined Chrysanthemums are placed in alternating-color strip of triangles.

Chrysanthemum Variation in a Triangle C

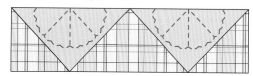

Two joined Chrysanthemums are placed in plain triangles alternated with plaid triangles.

Fans

I went even further and found a simple fan design to use for those who don't like stitching the scallops on Chrysanthemum. The fan can be substituted in any of the Chrysanthemum designs.

Fan Variation A

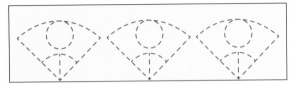

Fans in a row in rectangle

Fan Variation B

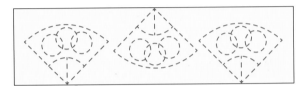

Fans alternated in rectangle

Fan Variation C

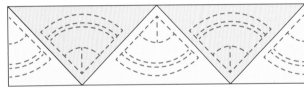

- Pieced rectangle made up of two different color triangles alternated
- Fans in both colors of triangles
- Right angle of fans at right angle of triangles

Fan Variation D

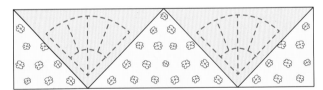

- Pieced rectangle made up of print and solid triangles
- Fans in solid triangles

Fan Variation E

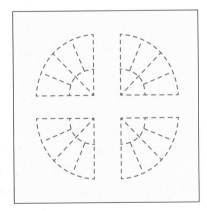

Four nonjoined fans radiating from square's center

Once I got started, it was amazing how many design variations I could create. I'm sure you can think of even more possibilities.

Gallery

Barcelona Twist

Kaffe Fassett designed the perfect tile print for this quilt to commemorate a trip to Spain. The pattern, Around the Twist, is not a repeat block design but rather a continuously pieced pattern. I had to take that into consideration in coming up with a simple quilting design that could be easily stitched.

Mary's Adirondack Baskets

A wooden inlay design on an antique cabinet door inspired this quilt. It is pieced with Japanese and Dutch stripe fabrics. The baskets are quilted simply by following the striped chevron pattern; a decorative stitch enhances the handles. The outer borders provide an opportunity for fancy cables, but even the inner borders could be enhanced with diagonal straight stitching.

Beamish Woman

A vintage photo printed on fabric at the Beamish Living History Museum in Great Britain was paired with reproduction prints from a quilt in the Victoria and Albert Museum. They made the perfect souvenir from a trip to the British Isles. I even worked in an inner border made from partial Circle within a Circle blocks. Learn to look for travel souvenirs that could be used on a quilt to commemorate your trip.

Bouquet for Gloria

A vintage bouquet panel designed by Gloria Vanderbilt in the 1970s was the starting point for this quilt. I had fun adding crochet motifs, buttons, French knots, and even a doily and a glove. To make it all square, I added a border pieced from partial Circle Within a Circle blocks cut from 1970s fabrics and feed sacks after adding scraps to the sides of panel.

Thank You Mood

It's always fun to visit places we have seen on our favorite TV programs. Mood Fabrics in New York City is a destination for Project Runway fans. The store's quilting section is where I found the perfect circle print for an alternate block to combine with Circle Within a Circle blocks. The pieced blocks were cut from Kaffe Fassett stripes and from shot cottons and overdyed dots from Wendy Richardson.

Christmas Curved Bowtie

Curved outer edges set this Bow Tie block apart from other simple Bow Tie blocks and make curved sashing necessary. In the center, I placed a dimensional biscuit puff, rather than an ordinary unpieced square. It's fun to see what you can do with holiday fabrics.

Curved Bowtie 2

A fabric swatch book from Robert Kaufman provided multiple colorways of the same dot print for the blocks. I selected Kaffe Fassett's Targets print for the border. A guide attached to the walking foot and run along the curved sashing made for quick border quilting.

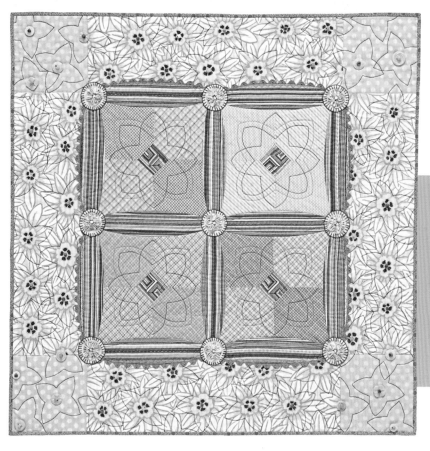

Curved Bowtie 3

Homespun fabrics were used for the blocks. Kaffe Fassett's Potenilla print was used for the border. The daisylike flower has a lot of petals, but a four-petal quilt motif gives the idea and stitches more quickly.

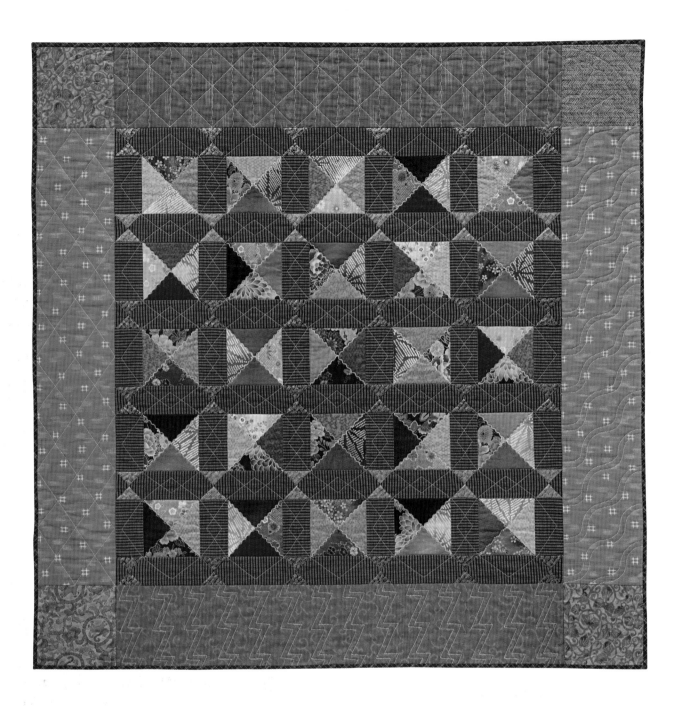

Japanese Treasure Chest

The simple blocks of this quilt let me show off a wide assortment of reproduction Japanese prints. The four borders and four corners presented an opportunity to stretch and come up with my own versions of traditional sashiko stitching designs translated to walking-foot machine quilting.

Sampler Quilt

The block is called either Robbing Peter to Pay Paul or Snowball. A quilt doesn't have to be large for you to learn a lot about creating quilting designs. I challenged myself to come up with a different quilting design for each block, each corner, and each border. The star shapes were all paper folded, but the circles were drawn from commercial templates.

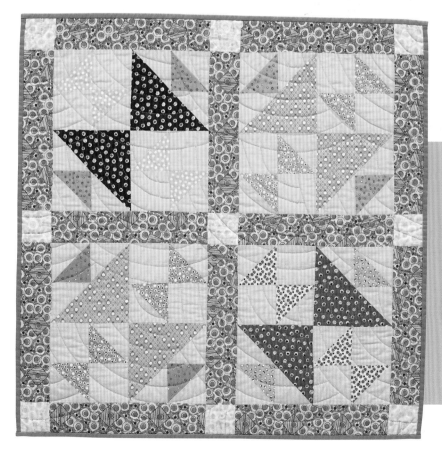

Not So Many Dots

Not So Many Dots was an opportunity for me to use 1930s reproduction dot fabrics, including an art deco one for the sashing. Peach background fabric sets off the triangles in the Old Maid's Puzzle block. Peach was a lot more exciting than muslin would have been. The seams were all pressed open so the top would lie flat, as I knew I was going to quilt with the allover Baptist Fan design.

Black and White Dot Pizza

My asymmetrical Pizza block is simple, and I use it often. I showcased black and white dots for the important large triangles and alternated red and blue dots for the block borders. The negative space is filled with multiple colorways of a dot fabric from a Robert Kaufman swatch book. The fun border fabric provided an opportunity for machine quilting, hand quilting, and button embellishment.

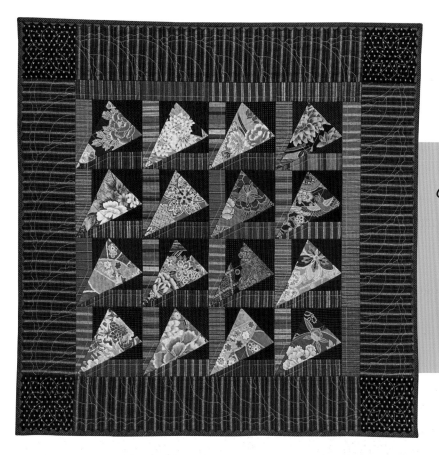

Japanese Pizza I

Reproduction Japanese florals are used for the large triangles. The blocks are bordered with a variety of red and orange Japanese stripes. The block quilting is straightforward and simple, but the striped outer border has a variation of Baptist Fan quilting that includes a decorative stitch.

Japanese Pizza II

Another layout variation presented itself for this quilt, which still uses the same prints and stripes for the blocks as Japanese Pizza I. The large triangles are quilted with a fancier design, which takes more skill and time. The outer border has a woven print with another Baptist Fan variation.

Indian Pizza

I used Usha Berlin's wonderful hand block–printed fabrics (handloombatik.com) in this quilt. I selected a much more complex quilting design for the blocks than I did in the other Pizza quilts. I changed my focus to the intersections of four block borders where two or four block centers meet. A diagonal plaid border is background for a cable border.

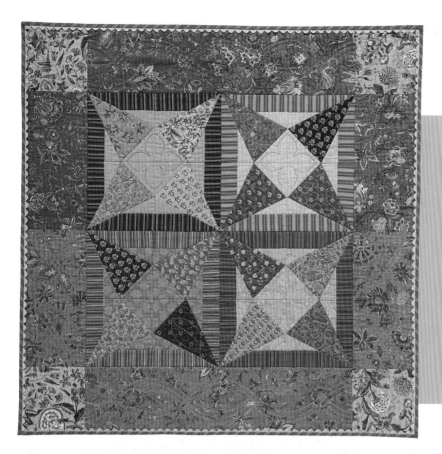

Dutch Pizza

Using reproduction Dutch prints, I tried
a totally different layout for this quilt.
Four Pizza blocks were joined to make
one large block. The four large negative-
space triangles form an on-point square
in the middle—perfect for a nice
quilting motif. I had four Dutch prints
to use for the border; however, the
pieces of fabric weren't wide enough
unless I pieced them. This gave me
the idea to make two-color borders.

Circle X

I have been experimenting with new
geometric shapes to use in my walking-
foot quilting. Sometimes a small quilt
is adequate to try out a new design.
This one uses a variety of fabrics from
the Kaffe Fassett Collective. Three
eight-point quilting shapes are nested
in the center. A small rickrack template
was perfect for the inner border.

Bouquet for Usha

A center panel is surrounded by blocks pieced from Usha Berlin's hand block–printed fabrics (handloombatik.com). The center is an example of a quilted grid used with appliqué. I had to do the diagonal grid quilting after stitching the appliquéd vase in place, so there were a lot of stops and starts around the vase. (Luckily I could add the crochet motifs afterward.) To make the grid more interesting, I sewed small clear buttons at the intersections of the quilting lines.

Long Beach Propellers

Sometimes the lines in a print suggest a perfect place to quilt. The border fabric told me "less is more." This is a good example of using a decorative machine stitch in a narrow border. I used an enlarged Bernina stitch down the center of the narrow stripe borders, which separate the pieced blocks from the beach scene borders.

Sayonara Gaigin

Japanese Boys' Day banners are hung outside the home on the day that celebrates the family's sons. Since they are hand painted, they don't lend themselves to fancy stitching. A simple design of lines and waves was enough. The Propeller block worked for an outer border, with the blades cut from many Japanese stripes.

Diagonal Serpentine Curves

I like simple blocks that can be laid out in different ways. The Serpentine
Curves block is a great example. Rows of darker Kaffe Fassett stripes
contrast lighter feed-sack stripes for dramatic effect. The fun print border
was perfect for both machine and hand quilting.

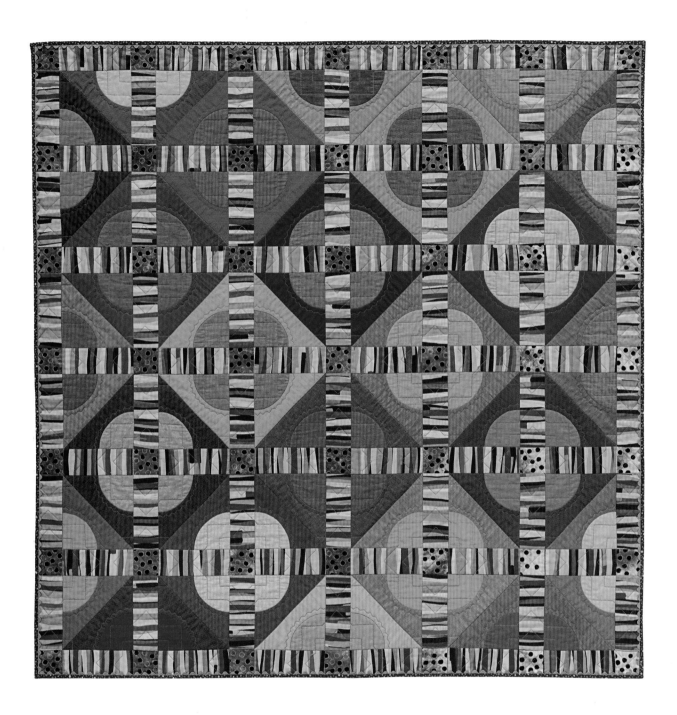

Sashed Serpentine Curves

I had never tried a traditional layout (blocks and sashing) using this block.
A little creative stretching produced this quilt. A great, slightly abstracted
stripe contrasts with solid-color blocks pieced from Kaffe Fassett's Shot
Cottons collection.

Fruit Delight

This quilt shows just how simple the concept of continuous quilting can be. Debra Lunn's hand-dyed fabrics contrast nicely with a black print background. The fruit print borders pick up the block colors. I tried different border and corner quilting designs.

Indonesian Swirling Petals

This quilt gave me a chance to use traditional Indonesian batiks provided by my sister. The overlapping quilting motifs in the blocks nicely fill the space where four corners of the separate blocks come together. A repeat diamond pattern print was perfect for the border.

Kaffe's Swirling Petals

A lot of Kaffe Fassett florals, combined with multiple colorways of one
of his stripes, made for a pastel-toned quilt. I used an enlarged decorative
stitch down the center of the inner polka-dot border and another enlarged
decorative stitch, along with the wave design, in the outer striped border.

Swirling Circles and Stripes

Emily Richardson's overdyed dot fabrics were added to Kaffe Fassett's woven stripes for the blocks. His Target print made a fun border. The colorway complemented the block fabrics. It was fun to combine hand-embroidered chain stitching with my machine quilting.

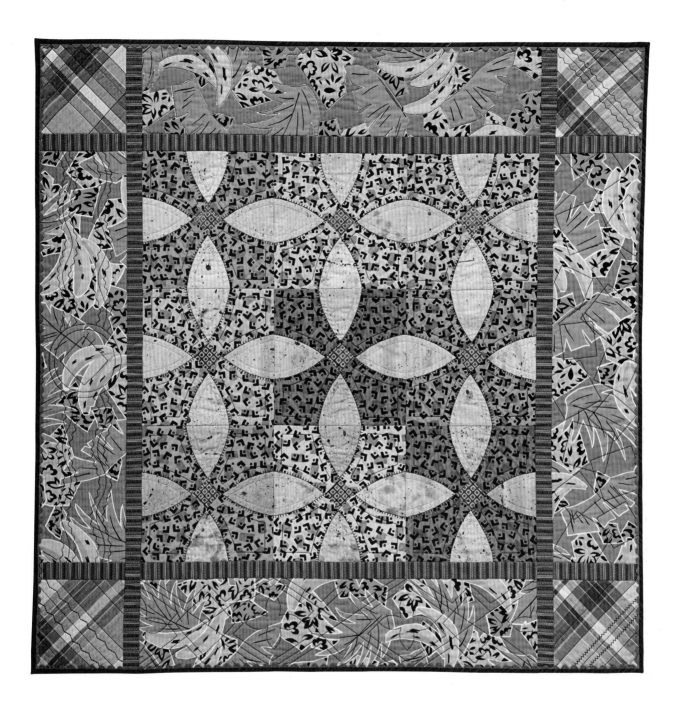

Tropical Delight

At last I got to combine fabrics that had been part of my collection for years. Debra Lunn was one of the first quilters to dye fabrics. Her overdyed print in multiple colorways was perfect for the Swirling Petal blocks. The banana print borders challenged me to come up with four different quilting designs, as did the plaid corners.

Wheels for Mary Bozak

Using scraps is the perfect assignment for the traditional Wagon Wheel block. With this quilt I honored the Hungarian grandmother I never met. The quilt combines traditional Hungarian blue prints, which represent her, with vintage feed-sack stripes, which represent me. I stretched the spokes to connect the blocks by carefully repeating the placement of the striped fabrics. Gingham yo-yos replace traditional center circles.

Wheels for Usha

More Usha Berlin fabrics (handloombatik.com) appear in this quilt. I challenged myself to come up with three quilting design variations using straight stitching and circles in different combinations for the three rows of blocks. Large yo-yos have buttons in their centers. Simple one- and two-print borders showcase repeated flower motifs.

Glove Quilt

Robert Kaufman sample swatch books provided fabrics in multiple colorways
for the center and corners of this quilt. They joined a border made from four
colorways of a Kaffe Fassett stripe. Real gloves, dimensional fabric flowers
I unstitched from a garage-sale handmade vest, and buttons were added to
make a playful quilt.

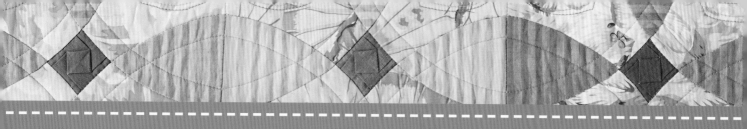

About the Author

Photo by BERNINA of America

Mary Mashuta became a quilter in the 1970s, when hand quilting was a common practice. She switched to machine quilting with a walking foot in the 1990s, which meant she could finish the many quilt tops she enjoyed making.

In the mid-1980s, she left careers in teaching and interior design to become a full-time international quilt teacher. Her classes have always included color and design work, but she has also emphasized what to do when the top is done. Because she never made the move to free-motion quilting, she has been able to help other quilters who are "drop the feed dog"–challenged. Now her students and readers know that they can finish their quilts without having to send them out for longarm quilting.

Mary's sixth book, *Foolproof Machine Quilting*, came out in 2008 and was well received. Now she has created even more designs that can be done with a walking foot. As a professionally trained teacher, she has also encouraged quilters to realize that they can come up with their own designs, from the simple to the more complex. This is an area where many would-be machine quilters need encouragement, as well as specific information about needles, threads, and batting.

In addition to her books, Mary has written numerous magazine articles. Her work has appeared in national quilt shows, including Quilt National and Visions. She had the fun of designing eleven quilts for the yearly book Kaffe Fassett creates for Rowan Fabrics. Mary is an ambassador for BERNINA of America. She lives in Berkeley, California, with her twin sister and fellow quilter, Roberta Horton. Together they were named the 2014 TQS Legends by *The Quilt Show* (thequiltshow.com).